How To Make
An Auth͏ ͏ ͏ ͏ ͏ ͏ ͏ ͏ English
Sun

With Yo
Roast Potatoes, Parsnips
& Onion Sauce

Geoff Wells

Authentic English Recipes
Book 5

Cover Artwork & Design by
Old Geezer Designs

Published in the United States by
Authentic English Recipes
an imprint of
DataIsland Software LLC,
Hollywood, Florida

https://ebooks.geezerguides.com

ISBN-13: 978-1976267932

ISBN-10: 1976267935

Table of Contents

DEDICATION

This series of books are dedicated to Mildred Ellen Wells 1906 - 2008

Mom lived for 102 incredible years. She went from horse drawn carriages and sailing ships to bullet trains and moon rockets.

She was not a fancy cook but everything she made tasted great. My dad grew much of what we ate in our garden so everything was always fresh and free of chemicals.

This book is a collection of some of her best recipes. I have just translated the quantities for the North American market.

I know she would be delighted to see all her recipes collected together so that you can continue to make these great tasting dishes.

Geoff Wells - Ontario, Canada - September 2012

INTRODUCTION

I get really ticked off when I hear disparaging comments from people about British food, particularly people that eat at McDonald's and spray cheese from a can. Obviously they have never eaten a real Authentic English Recipe.

I will admit that most of what we eat is not very fancy, we tend to cook mostly plain, good tasting, satisfying food. This series brings you a selection of downright delicious food that we Brits have been eating for hundreds of years.

It's great to try new recipes for the first time. To experience new flavors and food combinations you may never have thought of. But for most of our day to day cooking we never open a cookbook or precisely measure ingredients. We go by what feels right and the experience of having cooked the same meal many times before.

The "How To Make Authentic English Recipes" series is more about the method and the ingredients than it is about precise measuring.

Don't worry, I'll give you lots of measurements, (imperial and metric) so you'll get perfect results the first time. But after awhile you'll learn how to "wing it" and create great meals from fresh ingredients rather than packages.

This is the way our Grandmothers cooked and these are recipes my Grandmother passed down to my mother and she passed down to me.

I hope you enjoy the series and will soon be cooking like a true Brit.

The Sunday Roast

The Sunday Roast is a tradition in England both at home and in the pubs. Visit any pub in England on Sunday and expect to see roast beef, pork or lamb on the menu - maybe all three.

But as good as pub food is you can do better by following these simple steps.

Selecting the meat.

Although the meat is the main focus of the meal it is the simplest part to cook. Roasting is just applying dry heat until the internal temperature reaches a certain level. Because you are using dry heat you need to purchase the most tender grade and cut you can afford. The cuts sold as roasts are the most tender but the grade can make a big difference in the outcome of your meal so buy Prime if possible or choose pork which is always tender.

Lamb

If you will be serving lamb then your choice is generally shoulder of lamb or leg of lamb. For some reason lamb is not as popular in North America as either beef or pork and that's a pity because you are missing a tender sweet treat. Lamb needs to be cooked slowly, if you try to rush it, it can be tough.

Personally I prefer lamb shoulder but the leg seems to be easier to get.

Prime and Choice grades are all you are likely to see for lamb. Either can be successfully roasted.

Pork

A pork roast is easy to find and you can use loin, picnic shoulder or the fancier crown roast. If you are cooking a crown roast place it in the roasting pan with the bones down for the first hour then turn it over and fill the cavity with stuffing and continue cooking until your meat thermometer registers 185°F (85°C).

Pork is uniformly tender and is not graded so any pork roast is fine.

Beef

Of course beef is the most popular and you have a range of cuts to choose from. Most popular roasts are rump and standing rib.

Choose Prime or Choice grades for roasting as the lower grades will not be sufficiently tender when cooked with dry heat.

How To Roast

Basically you stand the meat in a roasting pan and put it in the oven. Not rocket science but it's amazing what can go wrong. A friend of ours inadvertently tripped the self clean feature of the oven, the door locked and she cooked the roast for three hours at over 800°F. Understandably it was a little over done.

A probe type thermometer is a good investment. This is the type you insert into the roast so you can measure the temperature in the center. I will give you some cooking times per pound later on but there is really no substitute for a thermometer.

We used to use a large roasting pan and surround the meat with potatoes, parsnips, carrots and onions but now I prefer to cook the potatoes and parsnips separately.

So the bottom line is to preheat the oven to 350°F (175°C, Gas Mark 4) for pork, 300°F (150°C, Gas Mark 2) for beef and lamb. Put the roast in the middle of the roasting pan and surround it with carrots and onions sufficient to serve your guests.

Stick your thermometer probe in the meat so that the tip of the probe is in the center of the roast and not touching any bones. Place the pan in the oven so that you can see the thermometer dial through the oven door.

Oven Roasting Beef

Serve with horseradish sauce.

A beef roast will generally be between 2 and 4 pounds (1 to 1.8 Kg). The various cuts are Inside Round, Prime Rib, Sirloin Tip, Top Sirloin, and Tenderloin.

If you can find it and if you can afford it, choose grass fed beef. There is a tremendous difference in taste that is absolutely worth the price. Cows are supposed to eat grass not corn and grass fed cows are not injected with all the chemicals that the factory raised cattle are subjected to.

Seasoning

Make some shallow cuts as if you were slicing the roast and rub in some of you favorite seasonings. Try mixing a little olive oil, salt & pepper together with minced garlic, dried thyme, dried rosemary and a little lemon zest.

Searing

Searing is the process of sealing in the meat juices by subjecting the exterior to high heat. It can be done on the stove top using a frying pan or in the oven at 450°F (230°C, Gas Mark 8). In the oven sear for 7 minutes per pound but no more than 30 minutes total.

Beef Cooking Times

Lower the oven temperature to 325° F (160° C, Gas Mark 3) and cook for 18 to 22 minutes per pound or until the meat thermometer registers 125° F (52° C).

Cover your roast in foil and let it rest for 15 - 20 minutes before carving. It will continue to cook and the internal temperature will continue to rise until it is cut. Final temperatures are-

    145°F (63°C) medium-rare
    160°F (71°C) medium
    170°F (77°C) well done

Oven Roasting Lamb

Serve with mint sauce.

The cuts of lamb you see most often are leg and shoulder. The leg usually has the bone in and the shoulder is boneless. Leg is more expensive than the shoulder but the shoulder is tastier and easier to cook.

Seasoning

A rub of rosemary and garlic is recommended along with salt, pepper and olive oil.

Searing

Remove from fridge 1 hour before cooking

Broil the lamb for 5 minutes or until the top of the lamb leg looks seared and browned.

Flip the lamb over and put back under the broiler for 5 minutes or until the other side is seared.

Flip the lamb leg over again and rub the top with the chopped garlic and rosemary.

With the bone in, a leg of lamb will be 5 to 7 pounds

> 3 tablespoons (45 mL) olive oil
> Salt and freshly ground black pepper
> 6 cloves garlic
> 3 stems fresh rosemary
> Roasting Temperature: 325°F (165° C, Gas Mark 3)

Lamb Cooking Times

Rare: 125°F (52° C), (about 15 minutes per pound)

Medium-Rare: 130°F to 135°F (55°C to 57°C), (about 20 minutes per pound)

Medium: 135°F to 140°F (57°C to 60°C), (about 25 minutes per pound)

Well-Done: 155°F to 165°F (68°C to 74°C), (about 30 minutes per pound)

Select a roast that is at least 4 pounds (2 Kg).

Choose prime or choice grades so the meat will be tender. Leg of lamb is most commonly available but shoulder is also a good choice.

Oven Roasting Pork

Serve with apple sauce.

Select a roast that is at least 4 pounds (2 Kg).

Pork is uniformly tender and is, therefore, not graded.

Roast at 350°F (175°C, Gas Mark 4) (for about 40 minutes per pound (450g) or until the internal temperature reaches 185°F (85°C).

Seasoning

My favorite seasoning for a pork roast is Basil.

Combine 1 tablespoon (15 mL) of dried Basil with 2 - 3 tablespoons (30 - 45 mL) of olive oil and rub all over the pork roast.

Searing

A pork roast does not need to be seared.

Pork Cooking Times

Pork doesn't have rare, medium and well states - just properly cooked. It is important that pork be sufficiently cooked.

Cook it at 350°F (180°C, Gas Mark 4) for 40 minutes per pound (450g).

The internal temperature, when it is fully cooked, should be 185°F (85°C)

Oven Roasting Poultry

Serve with sage & onion stuffing

You might want to consider a simple roast chicken for your Sunday dinner. I'm not talking about the full blown Thanksgiving/Christmas Turkey experience which I detail in my book "How To Cook A Thanksgiving / Christmas Turkey Dinner". - (http://amzn.to/2sQptze). This is a much simpler affair where you replace the beef, lamb or pork with a chicken.

Seasoning

The seasoning goes inside for poultry where it also helps soak up the excessive amount of fat in the meat. See the "Sage & Onion Stuffing" section later on in this book.

Searing

No searing for poultry, in fact you need to cover wing tips and breast with tin foil so that they don't dry out or burn. Just remove the foil for the last half hour of cooking.

Poultry Cooking Times

Always use a thermometer inserted into the thigh - but not touching the bone.

The bird will continue to cook a little after you remove it from the oven but before you start to carve ensure that the thermometer reads at least 165°F (75°C).

CONDIMENTS

MINT SAUCE (FOR LAMB)

One of my favorite things about a lamb roast is that I get to cover everything in mint sauce. If you have to buy it that's better than no mint sauce at all, but it is so easy to grow fresh mint and make your own.

It's best I say nothing about mint jelly.

Pick a few fresh mint leaves, then wash and finely chop them. Put the chopped leaves in a small container like a shot glass and cover with malt vinegar. Add a teaspoonful (5 mL) of sugar (or less) and stir. That's it. Just drizzle over the meat and anywhere else on your plate if you love fresh mint sauce.

APPLESAUCE (FOR PORK)

Jars of applesauce are easy to buy but your Sunday pork roast deserves better. Just finely chop a cooking apple like Bramley, Granny Smith or Spy, put in a small saucepan and add a little water - just a tablespoonful. Add some sugar or leave the tart apple taste. Boil for a few minutes until the apple is softened then serve warm.

If you own an Instant Pot you can also try the Instant Pot Applesauce Recipe later on in this book.

HORSERADISH SAUCE (FOR BEEF)

Store bought horseradish sauce is for wimps, even the stuff that claims to be "HOT" is mild compared to the fresh home grown variety. Of course if you don't like it, it makes no sense to ruin your meal just because it's the traditional condiment with beef.

For those of you that like horseradish, at least once in your life try the fresh homemade version. Horseradish is a root that is easy to grow or you can sometimes find it in a specialty grocery store. Use a vegetable peeler to remove the outer skin from an 8-10 inch (20-25 cm) long root.

Horseradish is way more potent than onions so don't touch your eyes without thoroughly washing your hands first. Even the fumes can be irritating so do your processing in a well ventilated area.

Put the chopped up root in a food processor with 2 tablespoonsful of water and process until well chopped. If there is too much liquid pour some off and add a tablespoonful of vinegar and a pinch of salt. Process again to combine the vinegar.

Put the mixture in a glass jar which you can refrigerate for 3 - 4 weeks.

SAGE & ONION STUFFING (FOR POULTRY)

Preparing a full Thanksgiving or Christmas dinner is more involved than the basic Sunday roast. I have included recipes for making stuffing bread and the actual stuffing below but if you want step by step Thanksgiving directions I urge you to look at my "How To Cook A Thanksgiving / Christmas Turkey Dinner". - (http://amzn.to/2sQptze)

STUFFING BREAD

INGREDIENTS

    1 cup (240 mL) water
    1 large egg
    3 tablespoons (45 mL) olive oil
    ½ onion, chopped
    2 teaspoons (10 mL) brown sugar
    ½ teaspoon (2.5 mL) salt
    ½ teaspoon (2.5 mL) black pepper, freshly ground
    2 teaspoons (10 mL) poultry seasoning
    1 teaspoon (5 mL) celery seeds
    2½ cups (300g) flour
    1½ teaspoons (7.5 mL) yeast
    ⅔ cup (100g) cornmeal

METHOD

Place ingredients in your bread maker in the order suggested by the manufacturer.

Select the white bread setting for a 2 pound (1Kg) loaf with a light crust. Press start.

After the bread has cooled slice it into ½ inch (1cm) thick slices and lay the slices out so they can get a little stale. You want the bread to be crumbly rather than moist. Cover the slices with a tea towel and leave them out overnight. You can also spread the slices on a cookie sheet and put the sheet in the oven. If they are not sufficiently dry in the morning just set the oven at 170°F (77°C) (lowest setting) and leave them for an hour.

Sage & Onion Stuffing

This recipe is enough for a 15 - 20 pound (7 - 9 Kg) turkey. You can alternatively stuff the neck cavity with sausage meat which adds some variety.

Ingredients

15 cups (750 g) of stuffing bread crumbs - (see recipe above)
1 medium to large onion
1 cup (225 g) melted butter
⅓ cup (5 g) fresh chopped sage (or 1 tablespoon (15 mL) dried sage)

Method

The size of your bread crumbs will effect the density of your stuffing. If you use very fine bread crumbs your stuffing will form a dense lump, if you use large pieces of bread your stuffing won't hold together. The best compromise is to use bread pieces that are a bit less than croûton size - less than quarter inch cubes. If you have done as I suggested and dried your slices of bread in the oven you can now tear the slices into small pieces. Take half-a-dozen pieces and rub them in the palm of your hands. They will crumble into perfect bread crumbs.

Add the fresh sage and chopped onion to your bread crumbs and mix well. Now add the melted butter and mix again. You don't want the mixture to be too wet as it is the job of the stuffing to absorb the juices from the turkey but you need enough butter so that the mixture holds together. Adjust the quantity of butter as required.

Fill both turkey cavities with the mixture and seal with skewers or use the plastic fastener that probably came with the turkey.

Yorkshire Pudding

Traditionally, in our house, Yorkshire Pudding was served with the Sunday roast. The roast came out of the oven to be carved and the Yorkshire mixture was poured into the roasting pan. It went back in the oven and was ready by the time the roast was carved.

There are no requirements that you do it that way but it does have the advantage of picking up all the wonderful flavours that are left on the bottom of the roasting pan.

The recipe for Yorkshire Pudding is the easiest thing in the world. Equal parts flour and milk (usually a cup each), an egg and a pinch of salt. If it doesn't rise properly, the next time try two or even three eggs but cut back on the milk as you don't want the batter too thin.

The secret to successful Yorkshire pudding is not in the recipe, it's in the method.

If you're planning to serve a Yorkshire, prepare the mixture early and let it get to room temperature. If you try to make it with milk cold from the fridge it is less likely to rise.

What most people think of when they think of Yorkshire pudding is a light, crispy and delicious sort of pancake. But that is not actually the original Yorkshire pudding. I had "real" Yorkshire pudding once and it is more like a suet pudding than what we think of today.

Ingredients

> 1 cup flour (120g) (either self-raising flour or all-purpose flour with 1 teaspoon (5 mL) of baking powder added)
> 1 egg (up to 3)
> 1 cup (240 mL) milk
> ¼ teaspoon (1.25 mL) salt

METHOD

Mix well and allow to rest at room temperature for a couple of hours.

Pre-heat oven to 450°F (230°C, Gas Mark 8) (after roast has been removed).

Use either the roasting pan or a muffin tin with sufficient fat (about ¼" or .5 cm) in the bottom.

Heat pan and fat to 450°F (230°C, Gas Mark 8) and carefully add the Yorkshire Pudding batter.

Bake in the hot oven for 20-25 minutes. Watch it carefully through the glass window of the oven. Avoid opening the oven door while it is cooking.

SUCCESS IS IN THE DETAILS

OK, let's refine my earlier recipe just a bit. Start with 1 cup of self-raising flour. Outside of England you're probably saying "What?". Self-raising flour is available in the US and Canada, but you might have to look for it in the specialty or imported section.

If you can't find it, don't worry about it. Just add a teaspoonful of baking powder to your regular, all-purpose white flour.

Beat a large egg and most of 1 cup (240 mL) of milk in a large measuring cup or bowl. Don't add all the milk because that might make the mixture too thin. Gradually add the flour making sure you don't get any lumps.

You are looking for a batter that is thicker than water but not as thick as honey. When you pour it into the pan you want it to spread to all sides but only just. After you've made a few you will know what I mean. So add as much of the remaining milk as you need to make the batter the right consistency

The idea here, as in all the books of this series, is not to blindly follow a recipe but to know why you are doing something and to make adjustments as you go.

Salt

Don't forget to add some salt. ¼ teaspoon (1.25 mL) is enough, but you need it as part of the chemistry of cooking.

Rest

As I said before, mix it early and let it sit on the counter so it will reach room temperature. It will still work if you don't but it will rise better if the batter is not fridge cold.

Cook It

It will take 20 - 30 minutes to cook in a 450°F - 500°F (230°C, Gas Mark 8 - 260°C, Gas Mark 10) oven so you should put it in the oven after everything else is done. Keep an eye on it so it doesn't burn, but don't open the oven - just peek through the glass.

Once it's done it gets cold very quickly so you want to put it on the plates just before bringing them to the table.

Two Ways

As I said in the beginning, your Yorkshire can be cooked in the roasting pan, which is the preferred way, or you can use a muffin pan and make individual Yorkshires, which Americans call Popovers. The advantage of cooking individual servings is that you obviously have more control over the serving size and they are less likely to fail.

Sometimes, if everything is not just right, a Yorkshire in the pan won't rise as much as it should. It can happen with Popovers, too, but it's harder to tell.

Hot Oven

Before you're ready to cook your Yorkshire, your roast pan or muffin pan should be up to about 450° F (230° C) or more. There should be a ¼" (.5 cm) of fat in the pan or each muffin cup.

The preference is for fat from the roast but any high temperature oil will work. Canola or Safflower oils are inexpensive and can take the high temperature without smoking too much.

When you're ready, remove the pan with the hot oil from the oven and put it firmly on top of the stove. Use premium quality oven mitts. You don't want to drop hot oil.

Pour the Yorkshire mix evenly into the pan. It will start cooking immediately but you want to get the pan bottom covered if you can.

Get the pan back in the oven as quickly and safely as you can.

I hope you have an oven with a glass you can see through because you need to resist the temptation to open the oven door to check on its progress.

Continue plating your meal and add the Yorkshire just before bringing the plates to the table.

Roast Potatoes & Parsnips

It just wouldn't be a Sunday roast without roast potatoes and parsnips. Some Americans call parsnips white carrots but they are only like carrots in appearance, the taste is much different. They have a sweet nutty flavour I'm sure you will enjoy.

Fresh carrots and parsnips are crisp not squishy. Be particularly careful when buying parsnips because they don't sell as quickly as carrots and some stores will keep them on the shelf well after they should be thrown away. If you can buy them loose so much the better but if you have to buy a bag look for parsnips about 1 - 1½ inches (2.5 - 3.5 cm) in diameter at the top.

Use a potato peeler to peel the parsnips then cut them in half so that you have a fat end and a thin end.. Cut the fat end in quarters lengthwise so you end up with five pieces all about the same length and thickness. Please don't take this too literally, I'm just trying to describe a process but it is not critical.

There are more than five hundred varieties of potatoes each with it's own taste and texture. You will never find that much choice in any store but you should try to choose the potato with the characteristics you need for the way you plan to cook them.

For roasting potatoes choose a low starch variety like King Edward, Red or New. You can also use a medium starch potato like Yukon Gold. Baking potatoes get too soft and tend to fall apart when you roast them.

Peel the potatoes and cut them into four to eight pieces depending on the size of the potato.

Allow at least one large potato per person and then add a couple of extra.

Any leftovers make great fry-up.

Parsnips generally come in a 2 or 3 pound (1.0 - 1.5 Kg) bag, so cook the entire bag.

CRISPY ROAST POTATOES & PARSNIPS

I like mine to be crispy so I cook them in a separate Pyrex™ dish which goes in the oven with the Yorkshire pudding.

For this method boil the parsnip and potato pieces in salted water for 5 - 10 minutes.

Drain them and pat them dry. Water will cause the hot oil to spit and will shorten the life of the oil if you plane to reuse it.

In a separate Pyrex™ dish (I use a 9" x 13" dish, (23cm x 33cm)) add sufficient oil (about ¼", 0.6 cm) and heat the dish in the hot oven like you do for the Yorkshire Pudding.

Using a kitchen spoon place the pieces in the Pyrex™ dish that contains the hot oil. Turn the pieces in the oil so that they are well covered.

Put the dish in the very hot oven with the Yorkshire pudding. They are done when they are golden brown which will be about the same time as the Yorkshire. About 20-25 minutes.

PAN ROASTED POTATOES & PARSNIPS

As I said earlier you can put the potatoes and parsnips around the roast or you can cook them separately. The result will be slightly different depending on your method. If you put them around the roast they will absorb some of the meat juices, which is great, but they won't get crispy.

It's as simple as arranging them around the roast about an hour before the roast will be done.

AIR FRYER ROAST POTATOES & PARSNIPS

If you own an Air Fryer you can use it to roast your potatoes and parsnips. I've included the instruction in a separate section later on in the book.

Onion Sauce

Onion sauce is something that is always served with the Sunday roast - at least it was at our house. It is super easy to make yet I never seem to make enough at dinner parties we have had, because everyone asks for more.

Start by peeling and cutting up ordinary white onions. Chop them lengthwise but as thin as you can - about ⅛ inch (.3 cm). One 3 inch (7.5 cm) diameter onion is enough for two servings so judge how much you need accordingly. If in doubt make more because the leftovers will keep in the fridge for several days.

Put the chopped onion in a small saucepan and 'just' cover with water. Don't drown them because you will use this water for gravy and you don't want to dilute the flavour.

Bring the water to a boil and cook for 10 - 15 minutes or until the onions are done. Pour off and save the water.

Now add enough milk to 'just' cover and ½ teaspoonful (2.5 mL) of salt to the cooked onions and heat the milk. Don't let it boil or it will boil all over your stove.

In a cup or measuring cup mix up some cornstarch. How much will depend on how much onion sauce you're making but 2 teaspoonsful (10 mL) should be enough for the one large onion in the example. Cornstarch should be mixed with as little water as possible - just enough to make it pourable.

When the onion milk mixture is very hot, but not boiling, slowly stir in the cornstarch until the milk thickens and you have onion sauce.

Green Veg & Carrots

Fresh peas, brussels sprouts or scarlet runner beans are the green veggie of choice but go ahead with broccoli, cabbage or whatever else is in season.

Whichever green vegetable you choose, remember, it only needs to be fork tender. Don't cook it to death, boiling for ten minutes is generally sufficient. Also, only use enough water to 'just' cover. You will be using the water to make your gravy, so you don't want to dilute the goodness.

Steaming

A better method to cook vegetables is to steam them. Pick up a metal or silicon steaming insert for your saucepan - just a couple of dollars at Walmart™. Put an inch (2.5cm) of water in the bottom of the saucepan with the vegetables on top of the steamer. Put the lid on the saucepan and boil for 10 minutes

Scarlet Runner Beans

These are very popular in England but never seen in North American stores. This is surprising because the Scarlet Runner is native to North America. The seeds are available in North America and some gardeners grow them just for their bright red flowers.

They grow very well in cool climates so are an ideal crop for Canada and the Northern States. The Scarlet Runner Bean is my personal favorite green vegetable and I could easily eat a plateful and nothing else.

Carrots

Carrots are a very underrated and unappreciated vegetable because they always seem to be overcooked - at least in my experience. Add a few to your steamer basket and stop cooking when you can insert a fork into them - they're done!

GRAVY

After you remove the cooked Yorkshire pour off any excess oil that may be in the roasting pan.

Scrap the bottom of the roasting pan to release any drippings or meat.

Add the onion water to the roasting pan and heat, on top of the stove, stirring to incorporate any juices from the roasting pan.

Add some of the green vegetable water to make the amount of gravy you want.

Ideally you will now add Bisto™ for truly authentic British gravy or you can add Bovril™ or a crumbled OXO™ bouillon cubes.

Add a couple of shakes of Worcestershire sauce. heat to almost boiling and thickened with cornstarch.

Don't forget to add any juice that leaks from the roast as you carve it.

DESSERT

For a truly authentic English dessert serve whatever you like just so long as it's covered with Birds Custard.

This is a family joke and I couldn't resist, sorry mum.

Actually this is time for a plug for some of my other books in this series.

I'm sure you've heard of English Trifle but you may not of heard of Fool's - at least not the ones you have for dessert. You'll find recipes for both in Volume 2, "How to Make Sherry Trifle"

You should also check our Volume 10, "How to Make Spotted Dick & Other Suet Puddings", which is full of all kinds of delicious authentic English desserts.

AND NOW FOR SOMETHING COMPLETELY DIFFERENT - PANCAKES (CRÊPES)

English pancakes are completely different to North American pancakes. North American pancakes are thick and doughy, eaten with butter and syrup and sometimes as a side order with eggs and bacon.

English pancakes are traditionally eaten only on Shrove Tuesday, are thin, crisp and eaten with sugar and lemon. In North America they are called crêpes.

This all relates to a book on Yorkshire pudding because they both use exactly the same batter. Except the batter is a bit thinner.

To make English pancakes heat a lightly greased frying pan to 325°F (165°C) and pour in enough batter to just cover the bottom of the pan. You will need to tip and turn the pan to get the batter to cover the whole bottom. Keep it thin.

Cook until the pancake releases from the pan and you can move it about.

Flip the pancake and sprinkle a teaspoonful of (5 mL) sugar over the cooked surface. Then add two teaspoonsful (10 mL) of lemon juice on top of the sugar.

When the pancake releases roll it up like you would roll up a carpet.

Pop it onto a warm plate and place in a warm oven 200°F (100°C, Gas Mark ½) while you make some more.

You can speed up the process by using more than one frying pan. It's a bit slow but makes a nice change for a Sunday lunch.

Check YouTube™ for pancake races that take place in English villages on Shrove Tuesday. It's a regular footrace with the twist that competitors carry a frying pan and flip their pancakes as they race.

TOAD IN THE HOLE

No Brits don't eat toads (most of them, anyway).

The "toads" in this dish are pork sausages cooked in the oven and surrounded by Yorkshire pudding.

Lay your pork sausages in the roasting pan then put them in the hot 450° F - 500° F (230°C, Gas Mark 8 - 260°C, Gas Mark 10) oven to start cooking. Take them out after 10 minutes and check the amount of oil in the pan. Add enough oil to bring the level to no more than ¼ inch (.5 cm). If you added oil put the pan back in the oven to bring the oil up to heat.

Yorkshire must be added to smoking hot oil so once you have it up to temperature go ahead and pour in the batter as I described above. Be very careful the pan is hot and you will feel it through cheap oven mitts.

When the Yorkshire is golden brown on the edges it is done. Remove from the oven and serve with mashed potatoes, gravy and onion sauce, (see the method above)

Air Fryer & Instant Pot Methods

I guess when it comes to these new fangled gadgets, we're a little late to the party, but they have now found an important place in my and Vicky's kitchen.

We use these new appliances so much we decided to re-release the Authentic English Recipes series with Air Fryer and Instant Pot directions for all appropriate recipes.

We have also added videos for all these recipes to our

https://instantpotvideorecipes.com

membership site.

As one of our loyal readers you get a free membership to this site as a bonus for buying this book. All you do is visit the secret claim page to get your 100% discount coupon code.

https://fun.geezerguides.com/freemembership

Instant Pot Roasting

Although cooking your Sunday roast in a pressure cooker may not really seem like "roasting", it still produces an amazing tender and tasty roast.

Technically, roasting is a dry heat process so it is wrong to call cooking in the Instant Pot, roasting but it definitely gets the job down and in a very short time.

Not only that, because you need to have some liquid in the pressure cooker for the pressure to build, you'll have liquid to make your gravy that's well-seasoned and tasty, too.

Times will vary slightly depending on the kind of meat you are cooking but the size of the "chunk" is the biggest factor. Cubes of stewing beef will cook faster than a single roast.

To be sure you can always insert a meat thermometer to check for doneness.

Beef
Rare [52°C, 125°F] • Medium [63°C, 145°F] • Well [71°C, 160°F]

Lamb
Medium [63°C, 145°F] • Well [71°C, 160°F]

Pork
No less than [85°C, 185°F]

Chicken & Turkey
No less than [75°C, 165°F]

Ingredients

3 - 4 lbs (2 to 2.5 Kg) roast (I urge you to pay the extra for animals raised in ethical conditions. Also grass fed beef is worth every penny for the wonderful taste)
Herbs to taste, such as thyme, rosemary, basil, etc. (I often use Herbes de Provence)
12 ounces (350 mL) vegetable broth (or chicken or beef)

2 cloves of garlic, halved

3 - 4 large carrots, peeled and chunked

2 medium onions, quartered

1 or 2 bouillon cubes, packets or liquid

METHOD

1. Rub the roast well with the herbs of your choice and let it sit for an hour or so.

2. Pour the broth into the Instant Pot, add the garlic, place the trivet in the bottom and place the roast on the trivet.

3. Close the lid, select the Manual setting and set the time for 35 minutes.

4. When cooking time is up, use Natural Pressure Release for 10 minutes, then release the pressure.

5. Use a meat thermometer to check the internal temperature at the thickest part - but not touching a bone.

6. Add the carrots and onions to the Instant Pot, close the lid, select the Manual setting for 5 minutes.

7. When cooking time is up, use Natural Pressure Release for 10 minutes and then release pressure.

8. Remove the carrots and onions to a warm serving dish and place in a 170°F, (77°C) oven to keep warm.

9. Check the temperature again but it should be done. (remember it will continue to cook slightly until you carve it)

10. Remove the roast and allow it to sit for 5-10 minutes before carving.

11. Add an appropriate bouillon flavor cube, packet or liquid to the broth for the type of meat you are cooking.

12. Place a tablespoonful of cornstarch into a small cup and stir in just enough water to make it pourable.

13. Click the Sauté button on the Instant Pot to bring the broth to a simmer and slowly stir in the liquid cornstarch.

14. Stop adding the cornstarch when the gravy is the consistency of honey.

AIR FRYER
ROAST POTATOES AND PARSNIPS

Roast potatoes and parsnips are a mainstay for English Sunday Roast Dinners. In England, parsnips are quiet common but not so much in certain areas of North America. You might even find that they are called "white carrots". However, they don't taste like carrots at all. When roasted, parsnips have a wonderful, nutty flavor. If you haven't tried them, you should.

Notes:

1. Be sure to use either Russet or Yukon Gold potatoes as they work best and make tasty roast potatoes.

2. Most recipes will tell you to peel the potatoes, I don't. Why? For a few or reasons: there's really no need to; most of the nutrition is in the peel, so why waste it; I think they taste better with the skins left on.

3. Make sure to cut the parsnips so that they are relatively the same size and thickness. They will cook much more evenly that way.

INGREDIENTS

2 - 3 medium Russet or Yukon Gold potatoes, scrubbed
3 - 4 medium parsnips, peeled

METHOD

1. Cut the well scrubbed potatoes into chunks.
2. Cut the peeled parsnips into 2 inch (5 cm) pieces. Halve, or quarter, the thicker sections so that all the pieces are about the same length and thickness.
3. Soak the potatoes and parsnips in cold water for at least ½ hour.
4. Drain them and dry thoroughly.
5. Pre-heat the air fryer to 400° F (200°C).
6. Place the potatoes and parsnips in a shallow bowl and drizzle them with the olive oil. Then toss to make sure they are evenly

coated. Optionally, you can spray them with olive oil using an olive oil mister. If you have no idea what I'm talking about take a look at this page on Amazon. http://amzn.to/2wQojJc

7. Place the parsnips ONLY in the basket and cook for 8 minutes.
8. Remove the basket. Shake well. Add the potatoes and return the basket to the air fryer. Cook for 10 minutes more.
9. Remove the basket. Shake well. Return the basket to the air fryer and cook for an additional 10 minutes. Both the potatoes and parsnips should be cooked through and nicely browned.
10. Serve immediately.

INSTANT POT APPLESAUCE

Applesauce is a great addition to any pork roast Sunday dinner. This is an easy recipe to make your own using the Instant Pot.

You'll find lots of applesauce recipes that tell you to peel the apples, I don't. Why? There are lots of nutrients in apple's skin and flavor, too!

Some recipes will also suggest sweetening the applesauce, I don't. Why? Apples are naturally sweet, there's no need to add additional sweeteners.

INGREDIENTS

6 - 8 medium to large apples (Granny Smith, Gala, McIntosh, Fuji, etc.), well washed
1 cup (240 mL) water
1 teaspoon (5 mL) lemon juice (freshly squeezed, if possible)

METHOD

1. Cut the well-washed apples into halves and then quarters. Remove the core and seeds then quarters into 2" (5 cm) chunks.

2. Place the apples in the Instant Pot along with 1 cup (240 mL) of water and 1 teaspoon (5 mL) lemon juice.

3. Close the Instant Pot lid and choose the Manual setting for 8 minutes. Be sure the steam vent is sealed.

4. Once the cooking cycle is complete, let the pressure release naturally for 2 - 3 minutes and then release the pressure.

5. Using an electric mixer or immersion blender to attain applesauce consistency. Alternately, you can place the cooked apples in a food processor.

6. Allow the applesauce to cool somewhat and then put it in clean, sterilized (running them through the dishwasher should be enough) mason jars and refrigerate.

   Note: Homemade applesauce will be okay in the fridge for about a week. It also freezes well and you can keep it in the freezer for up to a year.

BONUS ~ Claim Your Free Book

Thank you for buying this book! As a bonus we would like to give you another one absolutely free - No Strings Attached

You can choose any of the books in our catalog as your bonus. Just use this link or scan the QR code below -

https://fun.geezerguides.com/freebook

PLEASE REVIEW

As independent publishers, we rely on reviews and word-of-mouth recommendations to get the word out about our books.

If you've enjoyed this book, please consider leaving a review at the website you purchased it from

IF YOU'RE NOT SATISFIED

We aspire to the highest standards with all our books. If, for some reason, you're not satisfied, please let us know and we will try to make it right. You can always return the book for a full refund but we hope you will reserve that as a last option.

ABOUT THE AUTHOR

Geoff Wells was born in a small town outside London, England just after the 2nd World War. He left home at sixteen and emigrated to Canada, settling in the Toronto area of Southern Ontario. He had many jobs and interests early in life from real estate sales to helicopter pilot to restaurant owner. When the personal computer era began he finally settled down and became a computer programmer until he took early retirement. Now, as an author, he has written several popular series including: Authentic English Recipes, Reluctant Vegetarians and Terra Novian Reports, to name a few. He and his wife (and oft times co-author), Vicky, have been married since 1988 and divide their time between Ontario, Canada and the island of Eleuthera in The Bahamas.

Find all of Geoff's books at

https://ebooks.geezerguides.com

Follow Geoff on social media

 https://facebook.com/AuthorGeoffWells/

 geoffwells@ebooks.geezerguides.com

About Our Cookbooks

Quality

We are passionate about producing quality cookbooks. You'll never find "cut and pasted" recipes in any of our books.

Consistency

We endeavor to create consistent methods for both ingredients and instructions. In most of our recipes, the ingredients will be listed in the order in which they are used. We also try to make sure that the instructions make sense, are clear and are arranged in a logical order.

Only Quality Ingredients

To ensure that all of our recipes turn out exactly right, we call for only fresh, quality ingredients. You'll never find "ingredients" such as cake mixes, artificial sweeteners, artificial egg replacements, or any pre-packaged items. Ingredients, to us, are items in their natural (or as close to natural as possible), singular form: eggs, milk, cream, flour, salt, sugar, butter, coconut oil, vanilla extract, etc.

English Speaking Authors

We write all our books ourselves and never outsource them or scrape content from the Internet.

Published by Geezer Guides

When you see *Published by Geezer Guides* on any book, you can be confident that you are purchasing a quality product.

About Geezer Guides

Geezer Guides is a small independent publisher that only publishes original manuscripts. We will never sell you something that has just been copied from the Internet. All our books are properly formatted with a clickable table of contents.

Other Books You May Like

You can find our complete catalog at

https://ebooks.geezerguides.com

Plus Many More

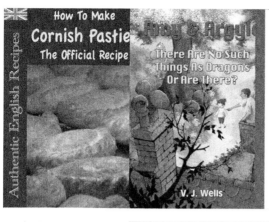

Plus Many More